It's Always A Mother's Day

A Dedication of Unconditional Love

EZEKIEL JEREMIAH

Copyright © 2021 by Ezekiel Jeremiah

All rights reserved. No part of this publication may be reproduced, distributed, or transmitted in any form or by any means, including photocopying, recording, or other electronic or mechanical methods, without the prior written permission of the publisher, except in the case brief quotations embodied in critical reviews and other noncommercial uses permitted by copyright law.

ISBN: 978-1-63945-181-4 (Paperback)
       978-1-63945-182-1 (Ebook)

The views expressed in this book are solely those of the author and do not necessarily reflect the views of the publisher, and the publisher hereby disclaims any responsibility for them.

Writers' Branding
1800-608-6550
www.writersbranding.com
orders@writersbranding.com

Contents

To Mothers 1
Mother Dearest 2
You Are the Greatest 3
Mother's Day Love 4
Because of You 5
Your Moment 7
A Guardian Angel 8
I Love You, Mom 9
You're Lovely 10
A Song of Love 11
To You 13
I Admire You 15
Loving Mother 16
You Are Loved 17
I Wondered 18
Morning Sun 20
My Heart 21
Love 22
Mother's Day Joy 24
A Time for Mom 26

Mother's Day Blessing...29
Live Life 30
Reflecting on Mother's Day 31
I Miss You...32
Today and Everyday 33

To Mothers

I honor you on this special Mother's Day. To a beautiful woman who has brought life to me. With love and devotion, you have protected me and raised me to be strong, proud, independent, and spiritual individual.

I am proud and blessed to have your unconditional love—a special love that glows through your eyes. Thank you, my beloved mother, for having me and keeping me safe and secure throughout the years. You are loved and respected, and I appreciate you for simply loving me. I simply say thank you for being you, for always being there, for knowing exactly what to do to put a smile on my face. I dedicate this Mother's Day to you. I honor you and love you.

A special dedication to my one and only mother, **Jean Reid**.

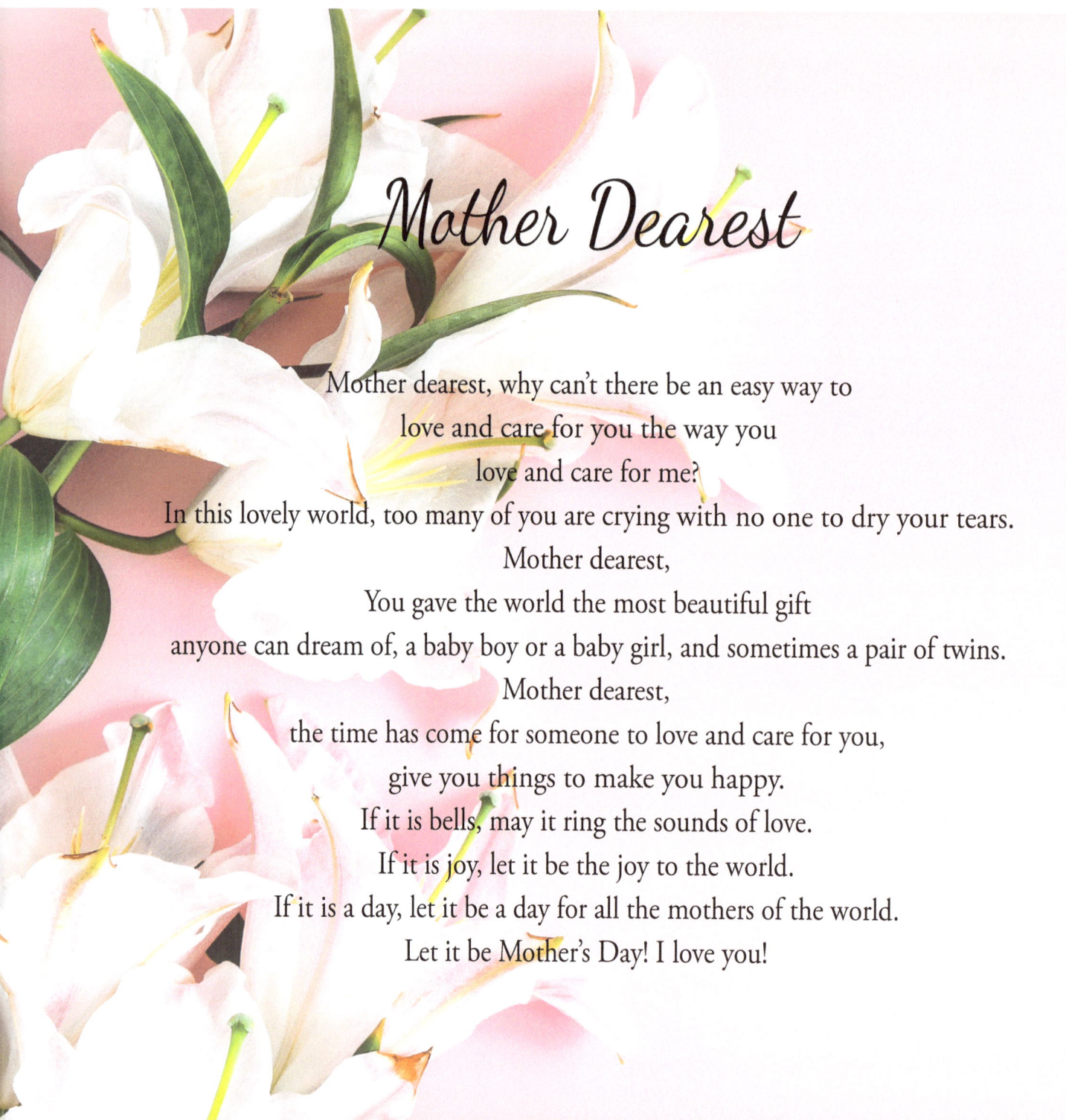

Mother Dearest

Mother dearest, why can't there be an easy way to
love and care for you the way you
love and care for me?
In this lovely world, too many of you are crying with no one to dry your tears.
Mother dearest,
You gave the world the most beautiful gift
anyone can dream of, a baby boy or a baby girl, and sometimes a pair of twins.
Mother dearest,
the time has come for someone to love and care for you,
give you things to make you happy.
If it is bells, may it ring the sounds of love.
If it is joy, let it be the joy to the world.
If it is a day, let it be a day for all the mothers of the world.
Let it be Mother's Day! I love you!

You Are the Greatest

Time and time again
we celebrate special moments and events,
which brings out the best in us.
When the little ones are born, it is a joyous moment.
How can we ever forget our mothers?
She's a monumental figure.
She stands tall.
Mother, you are the greatest.
On this day, you're simply the best.

Mother's Day Love

To celebrate Mother's Day is to celebrate you.
You have given me life, and only a mother's love
can bring forth such a beautiful being—me.
The nine months within your womb
protected me with your love and security,
along with a man's love I call Dad.
Two hearts joined as one to create a perfect me.
But it was you, Mother, who carried me
until I walked on my own.

We have been apart for these several years,
and though distances apart, we are still close at heart.
I came from you and I thank you
for loving me.

Because of You

Life is beautiful
like butterflies in the springtime.
The shining stars glow as they twinkle all night.
Your smile, like the morning sun,
shines so bright, reflecting a life well lived.

It is not your choice.
It's a gift from creation.
The moment you walked in,
I saw your beautiful face.
In it, heavenly grace.

Because of You

You only see a rainbow if you've also seen the rain.
When the sun is shining, life is so beautiful.
Like butterflies in springtime or walking by the sea's shore
watching the ocean where it meets the sky.
As the sun goes down, the world is filled with a beauty you can't deny.
Life is so beautiful—because of you.

Your Moment

Mother, your moment has come
for us to celebrate this day with you
for all the years
you loved and cared for me.
Words alone cannot express
the joy I feel
because of you.
I will always love and cherish the moments
with you.

A Guardian Angel

From the day I have known myself,
I have seen an angel
watching over me.

She made sure that I was loved and cared for
to the fullest.
She watches over me when I sleep
and is there when I awaken.
What more can I say?
Mom, you are my guardian angel.
I love you!

I Love You, Mom

Hello, Mother. How are you?
Today, I am sending you this card to wish you
all the best on Mother's Day.

I just want to say
thank you for being there for me,
to love me,
and care for me.

Mother, you are the greatest of all.
I just want to tell you from the bottom of my heart,
I love you, Mother. God bless and keep you always.

You're Lovely

Life is so lovely.
The way you live your life is a model of excellence.
The example you will leave behind
will last a lifetime.
You are like the tree planted
by the rivers of water,
bringing forth the sweetest fruit in due seasons.
You are more than diamonds and pearl.
Today you're on top of world. I adore you!

A Song of Love

Joy to the world,
that's what the people sing.
It's a day we celebrate.
We come together
to sing a song of love
for you, Mother.
A lovely lady—a queen.
The moment arrived
for the one who's alive.
Today, the sun shines for you.
Great God above declared a day especially for you.
Today belongs to you.
All the boys and girls of the world
join hands together,
singing you a song of love to say thank you.

A Song of Love

Because of you, we are all here.
So we continue to sing a song of joy.
We come together because we love you.
And to all the mothers of the world,
we sing you this song of love.

To You

Today as the sun shines,
its rays of beauty
brighten up the day,
and I always remember
when I was a child,
Mother, you walk me outside
and the sun was so bright.
You always tell me
the greatness of God
and how wonderful he is.
You told me about the stars at night.
You showed me the moon,
and when the moon is full,
you let me know it's a special moon tonight.

To You

I just want to tell you, Mother,
all those days and nights
you help me to be who I am.
I just want to say thank you.

Loving Mother

To my loving mother,
these words I send to you with love.
A garden of flowers,
a beauty sent from above.

As the river flows to the sea,
the wind reminds me
of God's greatness.
You, my mother,
is a gift from God
to the world,
so I can be here
in the present to let you know
you are a loving mom.
Thank you so much!

You Are Loved

Mother, your love is a blessing to the world.
When we see
the little boys and girls,
the future is secure because of you.

We always wish you the best of everything.
But in truth, words alone can't express
the true meaning of love.
So come give me a hug
because I truly love you.

I am happy you are my mother.
They say "diamonds last forever."
Mother, you last
generation after generation.

I Wondered

I wondered why
the stars twinkle at night.
I wondered why the moon shines so bright.
I wondered why the sun shines its light.
I wondered why
the rain falls.
I wondered why
the rainbow comes out.
I wondered why
the wind blows the breath of life.

I wondered why
the sea rushes to the shore.
I wondered why
the river rushes to the sea.

It's Always A Mother's Day

And then I knew—
because of you, Mother, I get to see this
wonder of life.
So, thank you for your kindness.
But most of all, thank you for your love.

Morning Sun

As I sit,
I watch the morning sun,
thinking of the time passed by and enjoying how it felt back then.
I also wonder about tomorrow,
hoping it could be like yesterday.
And then I realize, Mother,
we have now. So, let's just enjoy this moment.
Relish what it is to be together on this special day.

My Heart

Today is a wonderful day.
It warms my heart
to know that I was loved
by someone like you,
Mother dearest,
it is such a pleasure
to enjoy this warm
and welcoming atmosphere
with you.
I just want to share
this everlasting and cherished moment
as we live.

Love

A mother's love
brings joy to the world.
Her eyes are the pathway
that will lead us in life.

Her hands will hold us
in life when we cry.
Her lips are to teach us
as we are willing to learn.
Her nostrils are to
blow the breath of life.
This will keep the world alive.

It's Always A Mother's Day

Her hair is her beauty
A gift to her from the gods.
Her feet take us through
the journey of life
with God holding her hand,
His proof he left behind,
his footprints in the sand.

Mother's Day Joy

The joy of life
expresses its true love.
For its existence
in a time
when we celebrate
a day for our mother,
It too will express
the joyous moment.
That time is now, Mother.
Your determination
shows the compassion
for your ambition,
for life.

It's Always A Mother's Day

Your achievement
captivates me,
and I will be the first to say,
I love you.

A Time for Mom

The time has come
to show our love
for a beautiful woman,
my mother.

Who first to show me love,
who taught me the way of life and held me close
in times of need.
Mother, time and time again,
we show you how much we appreciate you
and love you.
Today, we take time out
just for you.

I Love You

A moment to pray
and to say thanks
to the Lord above who shows his love
and blesses us all.
All who can say
"Happy Mother's Day," it's a gift from God.
It's a joy to the world
to have a mother who is so elegant
and true like you.
A mother who is so daring
to take chances
to make sure her family
and everything is good and right around her.
I just wanted to give you this card, Mother,
because you are so special in my life.

Mother's Day Blessing

A special day for mothers is a special day for love
to enjoy with one another. It's surely a blessing from above.
Mother, you gave me life when there was no memory of me.
You gave me hope when there were no dreams.
The special things you do, like making things brand-new.
When I see little babies smile, I can't help but think of you.
You embrace me with your loveliness.
You cherish me with your kindness
Mother, I can't find words to express your gentleness,
But today is for you, Mother, I wish you all the best.
With lots of love, lots of joy, I love you, Mother.
Happy Mother's Day!

Live Life

You are a star whether you are near or far.
The breathtaking view with Cascade Mountains so high.
A moment of truth, a glance at nature.
Shadow by the trees as the sun stands still.
Its rays like laser aim between the leaves.
Mother, those are the moments I remember with you
while we were walking down the trail.
Such beauty lasts forever.
Now I can tell you such love lasts a lifetime
Because of you, Mother, live life.
A lot of love for you on this day.

Reflecting on Mother's Day

Reflecting on my childhood as far as I can remember,
I still cannot tell you anything about me while you were carrying me.
All through the pain, all through the suffering,
the struggle to bring me into this world.
Your strength and courage make you the most honored person in the world.
Mother's Day is golden; it is a joyous day.
Ruby, diamonds, and pearls, lots of roses everywhere
For only you, Mother, on this day we celebrate you
with love, with joy, and happiness.
This is my special thanks to you!

Happy Mother's Day!

I Miss You

Mother, more than you know
over the past years, I miss you so much.
The most difficult time in my life is being
here without you. I always miss your guidance.
Even so, you are always in my heart, and my thoughts
right at this moment, I'm thinking about you.
Because I love you, Mother; every day is special because of you.
I'm here, so today I honor you on this Mother's Day.
With love and respect,
Happy Mommy's Day.

Today and Everyday

Mother
Obey her
Treasure her
Honor her
Enjoy her
Respect her
`
Show her love

Do the best for her
A Mother is a gift for life
You know because you are here.